MW01656926

Manufactured in the United States

Published by Mrs. Jessie Brinkley and Dr. Alfred Brinkley
Courageous Expectations Consulting LLC, Publishing
Coexpconsulting@gmail.com

ISBN-979-8-9877289-6-3

Illustrations by Cameron Wilson for Soulsimplicity Design and Publishing.
For illustration inquires visit camdaillastrata.com.

WE ARE OUR HISTORY

History shows us all what we cannot see,
where we came from, and what we can be.
Wipe away our history and we may never know
why trees with no roots, frown and don't grow.
The seeds are all planted and watered too,
waiting on the sun to come shining through.
Help us to nurture the seeds that are sown,
connect us to our roots, let us grow on our own.
We are our history, there's more to what you see,
allow us to grow and become the best we can be.

–Alfred and Jessie Brinkley

WE ARE OUR HISTORY

BY DR. ALFRED BRINKLEY &
MRS. JESSIE BRINKLEY
ILLUSTRATED BY CAMERON WILSON

We are our history; my history is in me.

Statue of Liberty 1876

History holds the truth of how we came to be.

The Mayfower 1492

There are many stories of our history being told,
keep studying and learning about the days of old.

Trail of Tears 1838

Our past shapes our future, and history tells it all.

The Civil War 1861

Embracing it, we stand, but denying it we fall.

The Pearl Harbor attack 1941

History is a record of the people who were there, experiencing it, building it, and leaving it to share.

The Civil Rights Movement 1954

We can omit or deny, the mistakes that were made,
but history will never change, disappear, or fade.

The Holocaust 1933

History leads us forward and it confronts us too.

The American Slave Trade 1619

It shows who we are, no matter what we say or do.

The Women's Rights Movement 1848

WE

ARE

OUR

HISTORY!!!!

ABOUT THE AUTHOR

Dr. Alfred Brinkley and Mrs. Jessie Brinkley are authors, retired educators, motivational speakers, and educational consultants. Their primary focus is to Motivate, educate and inspire students to become successful in school and in life. They truly believe there is a successful child in every student.

In addition to this book, the Brinkleys have authored a total of 13 books.

As presiding officers and owners of Courageous Expectations Consulting LLC, the Brinkleys support and promote a commitment to volunteerism, self-knowledge, history and culture, self-respect, self-discipline, and personal self-sufficiency. To book or connect with the Brinkleys, email them at ***alfredbrinkley2@yahoo.com***

Made in the USA
Columbia, SC
22 November 2024

46664451R00015